BAGHDAD

Christmas

BAGHDAD

Christmas

By Bob Lonsberry

CFI
Springville, UT

ISBN 13: 978-1-55517-971-1
ISBN 10: 1-55517-971-1

Published by CFI, an imprint of Cedar Fort, Inc.
925 N. Main, Springville, UT, 84663
Distributed by Cedar Fort, Inc., www.cedarfort.com

Cover art by Glenn Harmon
Cover design by Nicole Williams
Cover design © 2006 by Lyle Mortimer
Printed in the United States of America

10 9 8 7 6 5 4 3 2 1

Printed on acid-free paper

DEDICATION

To all who have worn the uniform of the United States.

"IF NOBODY KNOWS IT'S CHRISTMAS," the SAW gunner said, "then it ain't Christmas. It's that simple. It's like the tree that falls in the woods. If nobody don't hear it, then it don't make no sound. End of story."

"Wrong answer," the grenadier said. "Christmas is Christmas. It just is. It's a date on the calendar, and if today's that date, then today is Christmas. And I'm telling you, Merry Christmas."

"Well ain't you mister good tidings of great joy?" The first man laughed. "Merry Christmas to you too, freak."

They had been together for three weeks, cobbled with two other guys into a fire team from bits and pieces that didn't quite make it over intact from the 10th Mountain. They were both PFCs, one from all over and one from Utah, and on this particular Christmas morning they were sitting in the rain somewhere ugly waiting for instructions. It was the two of them and the corporal and the specialist. The corporal was in charge and the specialist acted like he was in charge and that left the two PFCs to reflect on the fact that in the Army, the bad stuff flows downhill. And it was flowing pretty good right about now. Most everybody else was in the mess hall pretending to be amused by the sergeant major dressed up like Santa Claus, and the junior members of the junior fire team were outside in a Humvee reflecting on how crazy hard it can rain in the desert when it puts its mind to it.

The detail seemed easy enough—hopscotch a new radio from point A to point B while protecting government property and personnel and without getting into too much trouble with the locals. No need for a long parade—just a driver with a hotfoot and his fire-eating GI Joe pals to keep a lid on things. And the sooner they got started, the better, they figured. Get out there, get it done, and get back. And then get in line to wake up the people back home for a little bit of Christmas chitchat.

"If it's Christmas," the SAW gunner said, "then why didn't you get me anything?"

"What makes you think I didn't?" the grenadier answered. "Maybe I'm just waiting until the right moment."

"Well it better be good. My father sent me deodorant and insoles. Arch support and a pleasant odor—that's all I got going for me this year. It ain't quite a here-we-come-a-caroling white Christmas sort of Christmas this year."

He was kind of a thick kid. Twenty-four years old, a little short and a little heavy, he had joined the Army when he couldn't cut it selling cars. He'd been a night manager at a Denny's before that and had spent two fruitless semesters at the community college, and one night drunk after he quit the dealership he saw something on the cable about that plane that crashed in Pennsylvania, and sitting there with the tears streaming down his face he called his dad to say he was going to enlist. He got the SAW because he was strong as an ox and too proud to complain. And while he didn't think he fit in the Army and was counting the three years until he'd be discharged, he was exactly the kind of a guy you wanted in a fight. That's what the corporal said. Of course, the corporal really didn't know anything about people except how to move four of them in the dark woods of northern New York during a field training exercise. But this wasn't northern New York. This was the badlands and this was for real, and the radio had to get from point A to point B, and so he was inside with the specialist, going over the map and getting his last instructions while a couple hundred tone-deaf GIs in the mess hall next door were butchering "Silent Night."

The grenadier looked almost fragile. One of those wiry guys who's a lot stronger than he looks, a little tall, twenty-three, with a wife and a baby back home. A year of college, two years as a missionary, marriage to his high school sweetheart, and no idea how to make ends meet when she shortly thereafter turned up pregnant. He had to pay for the baby and he had to get money for school and he had to put a roof over his family's head. It was be fruit-ful and multiply meets by the sweat of your brow and, lo and behold, the recruiter had a plan. So he came into the infantry and got a bonus, and by the baby's first birthday he had orders to join the war on terror.

So far, the Army had been easy. He caught on to basic training the first day and just rolled with it. He'd already had some testing and some responsibility in life, and he knew how to put his head down and work. His first name was Spencer, but they had called him Pastor back in basic because he knelt beside his bed each night to say his prayers. At first it left the barracks with an awkward uneasiness, but after a couple of days two Born Agains asked if they could join him, and by the end of the week there was a nightly devotional in the dayroom with half the men in attendance.

But all the SAW gunner knew was that the skinny grenadier didn't swear. Not once in three weeks. Not even as they sat there with the rain pounding the steel above their heads.

"Get in the back, girls," the specialist shouted as he ran up to the Humvee.

He and the corporal were sprinting from the command

shack. Their hands were full, their M16s were slung across their backs, and they were trying to stay dry. The SAW gunner and the grenadier threw open the doors of the Humvee and scrambled up and back, out of the way, beneath the turret and onto the rear seats. The truck rocked slightly as the corporal and specialist jumped in and slammed the doors, the specialist behind the wheel and the corporal riding shotgun. The corporal unslung his rifle and put down his gear and opened his bag to hand two plastic-wrapped sandwiches to the men in the back. They were wheat bread around a thick slice of turkey roll, a smear of mashed potatoes, and two slabs of canned cranberry sauce.

"I made them myself," the corporal said.

"Thank goodness. If it was the cook I think we'd have had to shoot him," the SAW gunner said.

The Humvee had lurched out of the gate and driven half the length of the camp before the specialist looked over and noticed the sprig of mistletoe taped above the corporal's seat.

"You think that's funny?" he asked the men in the rear.

"Only if you do, specialist," the grenadier said. "Only if you do."

"Where'd you get that?" the corporal said.

"PX," the grenadier answered. "Never underestimate the ability of the Army and Air Force Exchange Service to transport useless crap to any far-flung corner of the globe."

Point A to point B was pretty much a straight shot. This was a routine run, not quite below the radar of operational concern, but not exactly the D-day invasion either. Everybody had to keep their eyes open, the specialist had to drive like he meant it, the townies had to cooperate, and the deed had to get done. On the far end somebody's radio wasn't up to snuff and somewhere in the big pay grades they had decided that the corporal's fire team could remedy that.

The road wasn't bad, but the Humvee rode like a beast anyway. Sometimes the soldiers thought that this was on purpose. They complained that they wanted the Eddie Bauer package on their next truck and that somebody needed to do something about the suspension PDQ. As they traveled through the streets and then out the other side of town, it was loud and hard to talk. That made the time go slower and left the men drifting. Not careless, but alone with their thoughts. A daydreaming vigilance. Thoughts of here and home, looking hard down side streets and on the roofline ahead but running through a list in their minds of who would be at Grandma's today and remembering the glow of the Christmases of their not-too-distant childhoods.

"What'd you get your kid?" the corporal shouted into the back.

"PX came through for me," the grenadier replied. "They sold me some footy pajamas—in a combat zone—and a sewing kit and a shoulder patch from the 82nd. I sewed the patch on the front of the footy pajamas and mailed it home."

"I never knew you were with the 82nd."

"I wasn't. But my wife's father was. He did some time at the Benning School for Boys, learned how to jump out of airplanes, and then went with some of his friends over to Vietnam to try to kill this guy named Charlie."

"I saw that movie," the SAW gunner said.

"So," the specialist yelled, "you got a twofer. You get junior a Christmas present, but what you're really doing is kissing up to your father-in-law."

"Well, I didn't get this far on my looks," the grenadier said. "Be nice to me and I'll let you see the little tyke this afternoon on the webcam."

"How about I take a pass and instead you get your wife to find me one of her friends to put on that camera."

"She's got a sister," the grenadier said. "You don't tick me off too bad and I'll see what I can do."

They were about half an hour out and had been quiet for some time when the corporal dug into his bag and pulled out a digital camera. He passed it back to the SAW gunner and asked him to take a picture of him underneath the mistletoe. The corporal twisted around in his seat, took off his helmet, smiled widely, and made a thumbs-up sign. He always did that. There were probably thirty pictures on that camera, all of them of that big kid with the same wide smile and the same thumbs-up sign. Each week he sent a few more home. Home to his folks and the girl he used to date and to a couple of guys who were on his wrestling team in high school. His mother had given one of them to the Penn-E-Saver, and they had published it under the headline "Local Man in War."

"Get one of me too," the specialist requested.

With his right hand on the wheel, he turned his shoulder to the right and brought his left hand around and made a sign with his fingers, looking gruffly into the camera as he did.

"Hey, no gang signs," the corporal laughed. "You going to put that on the cover of your rap CD? Is that for your homies?"

"Only if his homies are deaf," the SAW gunner said. "The specialist just told somebody that he loved them."

"That ain't for the company commander, is it?" the corporal said.

"No, fool. It's for my mom. She's an interpreter."

"Uh, specialist?" the SAW gunner said. "Don't you mean 'corporal' fool?"

They laughed and bounced along and the corporal said he wished he had some antlers or a red nose for the Humvee and the men in the back broke their sandwiches in two and passed half to the men in the front.

And that's when the RPG hit them—right in the middle of Christmas dinner. It sort of spiraled on a ribbon of smoke and hit the left front quarter panel, detonating against the engine and blowing the Humvee to its right, the front and top peeled half off by the blast.

The grenadier and the SAW gunner landed close to one another on the pavement, about a dozen feet from the mangled Humvee. The SAW gunner was facing the wreckage and immediately felt a searing pain where shrapnel had peppered his left leg. The grenadier was facing the opposite way, lying flat on his left side, his back almost pressing against the SAW gunner's back. For him it was different. There was no sensation. There was no sound. There was just the seeming fade up of consciousness as he saw flashes of light, three of them, four of them, maybe five, in a line on the roof of a building beside the road. *Rifle fire*, he thought, *rifle fire*, as calmly and serenely as he could think. "They're shooting at us," he said to no one. "They're shooting at us."

He could have been telling a waitress how he wanted his eggs. It was just matter of fact like that. "They're shooting at us." He sat up and pulled his gun around forward on its sling, and looking at those little flashes of light, becoming conscious now of the sound of rounds on metal and the flying dust and bits of ricocheting pavement, he reached forward for the trigger on his M203 grenade launcher and sent 40 millimeters of hellfire and brimstone onto that roof. Then it was like somebody pushed the fast-forward button. It was just all like a rushing wind, like a right now kind of thing. He came up onto his feet, became aware of the SAW gunner, and hunched down to see how he was. The shorter man said he was hit and it hurt but he thought he was good to go, and so the grenadier grabbed him by the vest and pulled him up, and they loped together the three or four strides to the impact side of the Humvee and hunkered down behind its wreckage.

Both men in the front had been killed instantly, but neither the grenadier nor the SAW gunner knew that. They were PFCs, for crying out loud. They didn't know anything. It wasn't their job to know anything. They were men under orders. American GIs. Junior-enlisted types. The guys the Army normally has buff the floors. Their job is to march in step and do push-ups. One guy from all over and one guy from Utah, and there's smoke coming out of the Humvee, and the corporal and the specialist are broken up bad, and right here and now the United States of America comes down to just two guys. Two guys in the badlands, and the flashes of light are coming back.

The grenadier threw off a burst of three, and the SAW gunner looked up and down the street. The RPG had come from the left and the rifle fire was coming from the right, and the grenadier fired again, and almost simultaneously he and the SAW gunner pointed to a building off away from the road on the left, in the center of a lot, hard to get to but easy to defend. "Let's head for there!"

The grenadier counted to three, arched the M203 into the middle of the muzzle blasts, and stood to pop bursts as the dust settled. The SAW gunner heard "three" and reached bodily across to the corporal and, grabbing him by his web gear, pulled him up and out of his seat and across the wreckage to the pavement, all the while saying, "You're going to be okay. Just stay with me. It looks pretty good. We're going to get you fixed up in a jiffy. You're doing okay, buddy." That's what they trained him to say, in basic and since. Everybody's okay in the Army.

"Don't worry, buddy, you're looking fine. I've got you now. I'm going to take care of you." In the civilian world emergency workers are told not to comment on your condition. But in the Army they keep it upbeat. They figure even a dying man deserves hope. Everybody's okay in the Army. By now the specialist was out of the Humvee lying on the pavement about two feet away from the corporal. The grenadier had gathered the two M16s that had been in the front of the Humvee and tried to pull out the SAW, but it was too entangled in the shredded truck.

"I'm ready," the SAW gunner said.

"Okay," the grenadier said. "Me too. On my three. One. Two. Three."

And the strangest thing happened. These two back-seat men acted like Audie Murphy. It was a ballet, a slow-motion firestorm—a stunning display of what you can do when you have to. A stunning display of what you can do when you're an American. The SAW gunner stood between the corporal and the specialist, one hand grasping the vest of one, the other hand grasping the vest of the other, and, on three, he began running, bent over forward, dragging their lifeless bodies to the side of the road and across the open lot toward the building. "It's okay, buddy, you're going to be all right. I've got you. You're going to be fine." There were three blood trails as he ran—his and the two men's—but the short, heavy man never faltered.

The grenadier followed him, walking backward, swinging his gun from side to side, firing the grenade launcher and the rifle intermittently, spraying the top of the building where the flashes of light had been, and pushing back some men who had come running behind a fence. One man dragged their comrades, the other man covered their retreat, a dozen men cowered in fear. A dozen or maybe more. That was the hard part. He knew he needed to count them, to get an idea of how many there were, but mostly it was just movement the grenadier was looking for—things that moved. If it moved he was going to shoot it. If he thought it was going to move he was going to shoot it. It was a time of great urgency and great calm. It was all very simple, really. The world was this one task. They were trying to shoot him, and he was trying to shoot them. It all came down to who did what to whom first. And as he walked backward and scanned the street, he heard the steady assurances of the SAW gunner to the dead men he dragged: "You're going to be okay."

The building was some kind of a store. A little general store. Two rooms. One big one with a few shelves of merchandise and a smaller one in the rear with a desk and a bed and a toilet. It was cinder block with two wide windows in the front and one metal door that was locked but which the grenadier was able to kick open fairly easily. They ran in and closed the door behind them and fell down in the middle of the floor, breathing hard. One turned to the corporal and the other turned to the specialist, and in a moment they found no radial pulse and no carotid pulse. They clumsily pulled off the fallen men's helmets and, acting independently and obliviously, they cranked the men's heads back and opened an airway and put in two rescue breaths and watched for chest rise and fall. The corporal's chest responded but the specialist's had been torn open, and the grenadier and the SAW gunner checked for neck pulses and found none, and the grenadier asked, "Is it two and fifteen?" And the SAW gunner said, "I think so." And when they pushed down they both felt the crunch of breaking ribs.

Fifteen compressions and two breaths. Fifteen compressions and two breaths. Fifteen compressions and two breaths. It was a frantic effort. They counted out loud. They both cried. They both prayed. They both tired. Minutes seemed to pass. And then there was the sharp report of rifle fire, and the grenadier said, "Take him," and the SAW gunner moved over between the men, kneeling, pressing down on the center of their chests with the palms of his hands while the grenadier scrambled to the big window and looked out for the locals. A round hit the glass and then another, and most of it fell out. The grenadier popped up and returned fire. Eight men with rifles, Kalashnikovs, were running abreast across the road, heading for the lot that surrounded the store where the Americans were holed up.

"I need some help," the grenadier said. "There's too many."

"On my three," he heard from beside the other window. "One. Two. Three."

None of the eight men took more than three more steps. They all fell, wounded or dead, strewn across the near side of the road and in the lot. As they fell, the grenadier and the SAW gunner ducked back down behind the cinder block wall of the store and sat with their backs against it.

"I think they're dead," the SAW gunner said.

"Yeah," the grenadier agreed. "I know I hit four of them for sure."

"No. I meant those two. The corporal and the specialist. I think they're dead."

"Yeah," the grenadier said. "I think they are."

It was an auto parts store, with canned foods and shoes and what looked like bags of animal feed. They sat there in the silence. It started to rain again, and a slight breeze blew through the shattered windows. The grenadier pulled the empty magazine out of his M16 and replaced it.

"What are we going to do?" the SAW gunner said.

"I don't know," the grenadier replied frankly. "I think probably we should stay here and wait for help. They'll come after us pretty soon."

"So it's kind of like a race?" the SAW gunner said. "If the good guys get here first we go home. If the bad guys get here first we get killed? We just wait?"

"I guess. I can't think of anything else, can you?"

He couldn't because there wasn't anything else to do. They were in a bad situation and that was just the way it was. And there was a complicating factor. The SAW gunner's left leg. Peppered with shrapnel, it had been oozing since the attack. Even now, leaning against the wall, he was sitting in the wetness of his own blood. But oddly he was unaware of it. It had hurt intensely at the beginning, when he was lying there on the pavement. But when they had begun moving, and as he had labored to save their two comrades during the firefight, he had lost awareness of it. Not just that it didn't hurt anymore, but also that he seemed oblivious to the fact that he was even injured.

And so he was startled when the grenadier started cutting away his pant leg to expose the wound.

"How's it look?" the SAW gunner asked.

"Not too bad," the grenadier said. "It looks pretty good. You're going to be okay."

Then he started tying pressure bandages and absorption pads onto the wounds and dragged over a couple of bags of animal feed.

"I've got an idea," the grenadier said. "How about

you lay down and I put your legs up onto these bags?"

"I thought you said I was all right?"

"You are. It's just a precaution. This is what we're supposed to do."

And so the grenadier grabbed the SAW gunner under the arms and turned him so that he was parallel to the wall, pushed up against it, lying flat on the floor with his feet on the feed bags. Then he put the man's M16 on his right side and gave him a couple of grenades and went back to his own position, where he could watch out the window and make sure no one was coming.

"Some Christmas, huh?" the SAW gunner said.

"It sure hasn't gone the way I would have hoped."

"Looks like you're going to be late for that webcam date."

"Yeah," the grenadier said. "Maybe I am."

There was a long period of silence. Then the wounded man spoke.

"Do you think that maybe you'll never see them again? I'm not trying to be a jerk, but just in your thinking. I mean, we're in a war. Do you ever think that maybe you'll never see them again? I mean, what if something happens and you don't make it out of here?"

It was one of those questions that are really about the guy doing the asking. "What do you think?" really means, "What should I think?" Maybe more to the point, it means, "I'm scared." Or, "Help me."

And it hurt the grenadier because he thought about

it every day. He loved his wife and he loved his baby, and he missed them almost as much as he could bear. And he knew what happened in war, and he knew what had happened to the two men lying on the floor in the center of the store, and he knew what kind of a situation he was in, and he knew what could happen to him. He knew all that. But that's not all he knew.

"No," he answered. "I never think that. I know I will see them again. I know with all my heart that I will see them and be with them again. I am certain of it."

"How can you know that? You can hope that. You can want that really bad. But how can you know that? Can't nobody know that, can they?"

"Actually," the grenadier said, "everybody can know that. Knowing that, for me, is the only thing that makes life worthwhile. I will see them again. It may not be in this life, but I will see them again. I have that promise from God. We will be reunited and we will be a family forever, no matter what."

"I wish I believed that. I'm not saying it's not true, I'm just saying I think I wish it, but I don't really believe it. When my mother died, everybody said I'd see her again in heaven, but I don't know about that stuff. I'm not really a religious guy. I don't know about those things. I want to believe it, but I think maybe it's fairy tales people make up because they're afraid of dying."

"It's not fairy tales. It's the truth. There is a God, he made us, he has a Son, and that Son came to redeem us.

That's the first thing you have to believe. It all comes back to faith in Christ. There is a God. Jesus is his Son. Jesus is our Savior. You can't believe anything until you believe that."

"I don't know. I don't think me and Jesus have been very good pals. I ain't been the best kind of man, you know. I've never been churchy. Me and the big guy ain't been close."

"That's not true," the grenadier said. "Listen, I'm going to tell you something, just between you and me, sitting here seeing what we see. I don't have anything to lose and neither do you, so I'm just going to tell you exactly what's in my heart. And you can believe it or not, it's up to you, but I want you to know that I'm certain it's true.

"The truth is that you and Jesus have been close. The truth is that you have fought for him and you have fought beside him. You have been brothers, and he still watches over you. Nothing happens that he doesn't know or care about. And right now, here where we are, he sees us and he cares about us."

"Then why don't he save us?"

"Maybe he will. Maybe he will and maybe he won't. But either way, his hand will be in it, and it will be for our best good. Things don't always work out our way, but they do always work out his way. And his way is the best way. We just have to have faith in that."

Out in the street a boy on a bicycle pedaled by. He

rode around the burned out Humvee and past the eight men lying in the street and the lot. He seemed not to notice or pretended not to notice or just wished he didn't have to notice.

"What's this all for?" the SAW gunner asked.

"What do you mean?" the grenadier said.

"This war. This whole thing. This morning. You and me here. What's it all about? Why aren't we back home right now with our families. Me and my old man, you and your wife and kid. What is all this?"

There were bolts of heavy, dark cloth on a shelf against the sidewall. The grenadier low-crawled under the windows and stood up to retrieve a bolt. Then, bending down again, he unrolled it and laid it like a blanket on the SAW gunner, who looked pale and was hitting pretty good on his canteen.

"Well," the grenadier said, low-crawling back to his position, "that's really a pretty easy one. It's about freedom. It's always about freedom. The kind of freedom you don't get for free. The kind of freedom you have to fight for. That's you and me. That's this war.

"And I don't mean just the freedom to vote for who you want or the freedom for women to go out uncovered or for people to marry who they want. I mean freedom of conscience. The freedom to believe what you want to believe. Freedom of religion. To really choose good or evil. That's what this war is about.

"Think about it. You got tens of millions of people,

a whole region of the world and not a one of them can wake up tomorrow and decide to be anything but what everybody else tells them to be. They're so tied up in traditions and rules that there is no freedom. The Bible says you have to believe in Jesus to go to heaven, but Jesus is outlawed here. That's not just politics. That's something more. That's the freedom of the soul. Freedom is more than voting how you want; freedom is praying how you want and worshipping who you want. But these people over here don't have that, and if we don't throw this yoke off them, it's going to spread, and someday our kids won't have that. We're out here fighting the devil. We're out here fighting the devil so that God's children can be free. Free to accept his Son and his Son's plan of salvation, free to decide for themselves what and who to have faith in. We're just giving people a choice.

"And it's an up-or-down thing. If you're not going forward you're going backward. There's no resting in this one. You can't make peace with evil because it never surrenders and it never relents. And it never loosens its chains on the minds and souls of men. Somebody's got to take those chains off. That's what you and I are doing. That's what you and I have always done."

"How do you mean?" the SAW gunner said.

"Well, I don't want to get too far into a Sunday School lesson, but we lived before we were born. Up in heaven with God. He was our father and we were his children and we were all there. And when it came time to make a plan for how things would be run down here, when it came time to figure out how, after our mortal lives, we could go back and live with God, there were two proposals put forward to carry out the plan. One involved freedom, the other involved compulsion.

"The devil was up there before he became the devil, and he wanted to force everyone to be good, to do what God wanted. He wanted a world without choice, without freedom, without something called agency. And everybody would get back to heaven because they never did wrong, and they never did wrong because they wouldn't be able to. They would not have the ability to choose evil.

"Which would have made us slaves. And that's not God's way. In God's way, we choose to do good, we're not forced to do good. According to God's way, we would have free choice, and that includes the choice to do wrong. If we did good, it would be because we chose to do good. The consequences were ours, good or bad, but so was the choice.

"And there was a war over it. Not a war of violence, I don't think, but a war of spirit and testimony and faith, and you and I both fought in that war. On the side of right. On the side of freedom. And we're back at it today."

The grenadier paused. It didn't make sense that it was just eight guys and no more. The grenadier was pretty sure that he had seen at least a dozen out there when they were coming over from the Humvee, and it wasn't likely the extras had decided to go home for lunch. Odds were, he figured, they were off getting more people or more weapons, and sooner or later they would assault the store—at which point he and a guy who looked like he was going into shock would be playing a little two-way rifle range with a bunch of ticked-off townies. That was going to be the game unless the cavalry came riding over the hill sometime soon. Sometimes it comes down to almost nothing—nothing but personal resolve and the American spirit. A man and his gun and his values, standing watch in the badlands.

"So," the SAW gunner said, "this is a holy war?"

"Of course. If it wasn't we wouldn't be here. You and me. If this wasn't holy, we wouldn't have come. We wouldn't have stepped forward. Defending America, spreading freedom—those are both holy things. The war in heaven followed us here, and our enemy—unsuccessful there—continues the same struggle here. He couldn't enslave people up there, so he's trying to do it down here. And we're taking it to him. And that's part of my religion. I have a testimony of that. That's in my heart.

"I believe America wasn't an accident. I believe God needed a place where freedom mattered, where it was protected and sacred. And he made America the torch, the flame that would consume the world. I believe God blessed America—that he ordained it for a special purpose, to be the protector and exemplar of freedom. And

America's job isn't done yet. Not while there are nations and cultures and religions that use force instead of reason, that chain people instead of liberate them. America's job isn't done yet. Our country isn't here just for us—it's here for the world. Not to be the world's welfare check, but to be the world's leader in liberty.

"See, if you look at the Statue of Liberty, she's not standing still. It's not just, 'Look at me, I raise my lamp beside the golden door, everybody come here and be free.' It's not that at all. Liberty is on the march. She is moving out. She is stepping forward, from America to the world. Liberty is to fill the world, to set its people free—to turn God's children free. And right now, you and me, in this uniform and on this deployment, we are Liberty's torch. You're dang right this is a holy war. And it's been going on since before Adam and Eve."

"You got anything more in your canteen?" the SAW gunner asked. "I'm a little thirsty and cold over here."

The grenadier slid his canteen across the floor and low-crawled along the center aisle to a small display of Pepsi. He knew, technically, that the caffeine wasn't a very good thing, given the situation, but he also knew, given the situation, it didn't make much of a difference. He slid several bottles across the floor, and they bumped against the SAW gunner, who was up on one elbow emptying the canteen. He was sweating in the cold but seemed in good spirits.

"Remind me not to do this again," he said. "I don't think I wanted a Purple Heart this bad."

"Oh, quit your complaining. Pretty soon you'll be in a white robe in the hospital and some visiting general will pin it on you. Then you'll spend the next fifty years telling people about it."

As he spoke, the grenadier was sitting on a case of motor oil, away from the window, in the shadows of the room. His elbows were on his knees, and the M16 was at his shoulder. He was looking through the aperture ring and over the front sight to a narrow gap between two buildings across the street and down a ways. He inhaled, let his breath half out and held the rest in, motionless, his finger gently on the trigger, his eye blinking twice to wipe away the tearing from the breeze and the staring. *It's the same way with deer,* he thought. *When you see one cut across the trail and you can't get a shot off, you cover the trail where it passed. You pick your spot and you cover it.* Ready, safety off, a hammer's fall away. *Because more times than not that deer's not traveling alone, and the next one is just a little bit behind.*

His grandfather had taught him that lesson one time up in Sanpete County or maybe across the line in Juab County, and one time—Bam! A guy darted across the gap, and the grenadier tapped the trigger. The thing on the guy's head lost its shape, and he dropped dead in place between the buildings.

"What'd you get, Pa?" the SAW gunner asked, trying not to seem startled by the shot. "Something for supper?"

"It looks like bubblin' crude, Jethro."

"The kin folks said, 'Move away from there,' and I think they were onto something. I think I'll move off to Beverly Hills and track down Ellie Mae."

"Two things," the grenadier said. "You watch too much TVLand, and Ellie Mae is ninety years old now."

He was still looking through his sights, sitting on the case of oil with his elbows on his knees. He didn't expect anybody to come drag this guy off, but he was covering him anyway, and he figured that that still left them with three and however many cousins and clansmen they had coming. And he remembered that in basic training the senior drill, a Christian guy named Bacon, got up in front of them at the range one morning, waiting for the ducks to get in a row, and said, "Someday it may be your day to die. But when that day comes, don't die easy, and don't die alone." And the grenadier felt like he was dress right dress with that. "I'm not going easy, drill sergeant," he whispered. "And I'm not going alone."

"So the whole point," the SAW gunner said, "is to run around free? Just do your own thing?"

"Actually," the grenadier said, "that's half of it. The first half is freedom, and the second half is using that freedom to choose righteousness. People must be free to be moral agents for themselves. Then they must be taught the truth so they can choose the right. Liberate them and convert them, that's my plan for the world. And I think that's God's plan for the world. We're all either soldiers or missionaries. Not just soldiers with guns, but fighters for freedom, however we do it, whatever our circumstance. And when people are free to follow their own conscience, then we set about to teach them."

"So what would you teach me?" His breath was shallow when he said it. And earnest. Not the playful challenging that was his nature. He wasn't being snide; he was being sincere. It wasn't a question so much as it was a plea.

The grenadier stared unfocused out the window as he thought about how to answer. For two years he had looked for just such an opportunity. Knocked on doors for it. Stopped people on the streets for it. And it had come in a dozen different ways, and there was a scrapbook at home with pictures of him in white next to this family and that family and a handful of people he could never forget. But this one made him cry. Just a quick burst of snuff-your-nose-and-wipe-a-tear-away-and-clear-your-throat-and-collect-your-thoughts kind of cry.

Then he spoke.

"'For God so loved the world, that he gave his only begotten Son, that whosoever believeth on him should not perish, but have everlasting life.'

"'And now, after the many testimonies which have been given of him, this is the testimony, last of all, which we give of him: That he lives! For we saw him, even on the right hand of God; and we heard the voice bearing record that he is the Only Begotten of the Father—That by him, and through him, and of him, the worlds are and were created, and the inhabitants thereof are begotten sons and daughters unto God.'

"'And now, I would commend you to seek this Jesus of whom the prophets and apostles have written, that the grace of God the Father, and also the Lord Jesus Christ, and the Holy Ghost, which beareth record of them, may be and abide in you forever.'

"'I glory in my Jesus, for he hath redeemed my soul from hell.'

"'Jesus saith unto him, I am the way, the truth, and the life: no man cometh unto the Father, but by me.'

"That's what I would teach you. I would teach you that Jesus is your brother, that he is your Redeemer. That he loves you and wants to save you. That he understands you, that he knows your pain, and that he can heal you and forgive you. That he has never left your side, and that he is with you even now. That he stands at the door and knocks. I would teach you those things and tell you that I know they are true. I know they are true because as I have thought and prayed about them, I have felt in my heart the warm and comforting witness of the Holy Ghost giving testimony that can never be refuted or ignored. I would tell you that I know that Jesus is your Savior because I know that Jesus is my Savior."

The short, solid man lying against the wall was weeping softly. His right hand clutched the M16 on the floor beside him; his left hand pinched the bridge of his nose the way it had when he was a little boy and his emotions had overcome him.

"Are you a preacher or something?" the SAW gunner asked.

"I hold the priesthood of the Lord," the grenadier replied.

"Then can you give me Last Rites? Please, I don't want to die if I ain't right with God. I want to know he knows how I feel."

There was a pause. Outside they could hear nothing but the rain. Then the Utah boy spoke.

"Sure. I can do that."

He low-crawled beneath the windows and worked himself around behind the SAW gunner and knelt at his head. He took off the man's helmet and put his hands on his head and asked him his full name. The man responded and the grenadier repeated it and said, "By the authority of the Holy Melchizedek Priesthood and in the name of Jesus Christ, I lay my hands on your head and give you this blessing of strength and comfort."

There was another pause, and the SAW gunner felt a quiver go through the grenadier, and a tear fell on the gunner's forehead. Then the thin man inhaled sharply and spoke.

"My brother, the Lord wants you to know that this will be the best day of your life. He wants you to know that he loves you dearly and that he is watching over you.

That he knows what it is to be wounded in a fight with evil and to feel the pains of injury. He has feared and wept and known anguish. He has suffered alone among his enemies. He knows what it is to lie broken and bleeding. So you are not alone. You will never be alone. You will never be beyond the reach of your Savior's love and power.

"The Lord invites you to come to him. To have faith in him. To repent of your sins. To be baptized. To continue the struggle for righteousness. To do what is right and defend what is noble. To be an example and a friend. To be a child of God. As you do this with singleness of heart, as you grow in your faith and obey your Master, you will grow closer to the God who gave you life and who waits to welcome you home.

"But today is not your day to die. Today is your day to live. You have been redeemed, and you may be exalted if you follow the path that you have set out upon today.

"Remember your friends, and honor their memory.

"I bless you with physical strength, that your body may sustain itself and mend. I bless you with courage, that you may endure the difficulties through which you will pass. I bless you that the angels of heaven will watch over you and deliver you home. You have been redeemed at the price of blood. Never forget that, and always be grateful for that.

"Your God delights in you today, and he is pleased by the sincerity of your heart. Keep this spirit with you, and all will be well with you.

"I seal these blessings upon you, according to your faith, in the sacred name of Jesus Christ. Amen."

The SAW gunner lifted his hand off the action of his M16 and extended it toward the grenadier, who took it and shook it. They muttered "thank you," and the grenadier low-crawled back to his case of oil. He sat up and surveyed the street as far as he could see in each direction. Nothing seemed to have changed but he didn't feel good about things. It didn't seem that it should be this quiet. They were massing, he figured, waiting for more men or more munitions or something. Maybe the cavalry was on the way, and that had them spooked. Maybe there was a line of heavy metal slinging its way down the road right now, intent on pulling these two out of the juicer and coming to settle the score. Or maybe it was shooting fish in a barrel, and the good guys were the fish.

"Must be that was the only RPG they had," the SAW gunner said. "If they'd had another one, they'd have sent it in here to liven things up a bit. It's kind of a smoke-'em-if-you've-got-'em thing, and if they haven't smoked 'em, I'm figuring they ain't got 'em. Which is all to our good."

"Yeah, probably," the grenadier said. "Or they're waiting until dark. That's kind of what I think. They're waiting until dark. It's easier for them that way, and they can probably get across this lot without getting fried. We lose sight, and we're going to have the whole kit and caboodle of them jumping through these windows. I'm pretty sure they'll wait until dark."

"Or until the good guys are ten minutes out," the SAW gunner said. "If it looks like GI Joe is coming down here to smack the townies, I'm afraid they're going to try to get rid of us first. These people count noses, and right now they're behind nine to two. They're going to have terrible self-esteem issues if they leave either one of us alive."

"Yeah. I think you're right. Their best play is to kill us and disappear into the woodwork just as the relief is rolling up."

"Then here's our play. You help me get over there against that far wall, and when they come through the door we'll just turn loose on 'em with everything we've got. It'll be a 'y'all come,' and when the dust settles we'll find out who the real men are."

"Couldn't we just settle this with light sabers, like gentleman?" the grenadier said.

"Nah," the SAW gunner said. "I'm more of a Harry Potter man myself."

"Now that's funny," the grenadier said, "because I always thought you looked more like a hobbit. Or that short guy with the lisp in *The Princess Bride*."

All of this was meant to avoid discussing the fact that the SAW gunner was about as far into shocky as a man can get. He was pale, sopping wet, not quite as alert as he had been, and if it had been polite to go over and check his pulse, the grenadier was pretty sure it would be fast and thready, the way it gets just before somebody crashes and burns. What this GI needed was an IV, and he needed it quick. But that was the one thing this store didn't stock, and it wasn't likely that the locals outside would drop one by as a welcome to the neighborhood. This was one of those sands in the hourglass things, when the clock can run out and the game can be lost.

"How about this," the grenadier said. "You stay where you are. When the bad guys make their rush, I'm heading outside with guns blazing. I'm going to pop off all these grenade rounds I've been lugging around, and then I'm going to see how fast I can empty an M16. I think it'll get really loud and will be bad for our hearing, but then it will quiet down. That's when you need to listen. If you hear somebody walking toward the building and he's speaking English, then the Pepsis are on me. But if you hear somebody walking toward the building, and he's not on the English-only plan, then you wait for him to get close and you right-hand one of those grenades I gave you out the window. You've got two, so you can play that game more than once if you have to. Stay up against the wall, and you ought to be okay."

"Are you sure?" the SAW gunner asked. "Why don't you put me against that wall in the back? That's where I want to be. Let me fight it out. Let me shoot some of these guys."

"Sorry, buck. No can do. I'm not letting you get all

the glory. Now, as you well know, Army regulations say that in the event that two soldiers of the same rank are together, the one who's taller shall be in command. So my plan's the plan, and don't give me any guff or I'm going to make you start saluting me."

So the SAW gunner continued to lie in his position, up against the wall beneath the window. And the grenadier took his place, on the case of oil, his M16 with the M203 in his hands, the spare magazines from the specialist and the corporal bulging in his pockets. And they sat that way for a while. Afternoon was wearing away and the street was still deserted and the rain had stopped. It was silent.

"Should we do something for Christmas?" the SAW gunner asked.

"Like what?"

"I don't know. Just something. It's Christmas. It means something. We ought to do something."

"Oh yeah," the grenadier said. "Like that Christmas tree falling in the woods."

The SAW gunner laughed and said, "Hey, I used to know that thing from Charlie Brown about the shepherds and the flocks. I could try to remember that."

"That'd be nice," the grenadier said. "That'd be real nice."

"Okay, it was something like this. 'It came to pass in them days that there went out a decree from Caesar Augustus, that all the world would be taxed. And all went to be taxed, every one into his own city. And Joseph also went up into Judea, unto the city of David, which is called Bethlehem, to be taxed with Mary, his espoused wife.'"

He paused.

"'Being great with child,'" the grenadier said.

"Yeah, being great with child. Hold it. How did you know that? Do you got all the Bible memorized?"

"No, but I do know how to cheat," the grenadier said, lifting his hand to show the pocket New Testament he had gotten from the Gideons at basic training.

"Okay then, help me out."

And they began reciting it together. The SAW gunner faltered, misremembering, and dropped out a few verses.

"'And so it was that, while they were there, the days were accomplished that she should be delivered. And she brought forth her firstborn son, and wrapped him in swaddling clothes, and laid him in a manger; because there was no room for them in the inn. And there were in the same country shepherds abiding in the field, keeping watch over their flock by night. And lo, the angel of the Lord came upon them, and the glory of the Lord shone round about them: and they were sore afraid. And the angel said unto them, Fear not: for, behold, I bring you good tidings of great joy, which shall be to all people. For unto you is born this day in the city of David a Saviour, which is Christ the Lord. And this shall be a sign unto you; Ye shall find the babe wrapped in swaddling clothes, lying in a manger. And suddenly there was with the angel a multitude of the heavenly host praising God, and saying, Glory to God in the highest, and on earth peace, good will toward men."

Then, from the floor, the SAW gunner began singing "Silent Night." It was an odd, unexpected sound, but the grenadier joined in by the second line. And together their voices rose until they were singing as loud as they could the anthem of Christmas. Not about jingling bells or snowmen or red-nosed reindeer, but about the baby Jesus, the condescension of God, the redemption of mankind. A song they had learned as boys, a song they clung to as men. On this Christmas day in the badlands. Then the grenadier opened the pocket New Testament to the page with the full-color American flag and, holding the book in his left hand, spreading its pages apart with his fingers, he raised it overhead and put his right hand on his heart. The SAW gunner followed suit, and up and down the street the sounds of men singing in English were replaced by the steady reciting of the Pledge of Allegiance. Then the grenadier asked the SAW gunner if he would say a prayer for them.

The SAW gunner was uncomfortable and said he only knew the prayer his mother said for grace and the "Now I lay me down to sleep" prayer, and he didn't know what to say or how to say it.

"That's okay," the grenadier said. "Let me tell you how my dad taught me. He had been a missionary back before he married my mother, and back when he was out they taught people lessons with a big black binder—a 'flip chart,' they called it—and it had all these pictures and visual aids. And he used to pull that flip chart out to teach us kids little lessons on Monday nights, and I can't tell you how many times he showed us this one page. It had four simple steps on it. Little phrases on how to say a prayer. The first one was, 'Heavenly Father.' The second one was 'We thank thee.' Then, 'We ask thee.' And, finally, 'In the name of Jesus Christ. Amen.'

"It's a pretty simple system. You're talking to God, so you begin by addressing him. He is our Father in Heaven, so we call him Heavenly Father. Then we thank him for the blessings he has given us. Then when we've said our thank-yous, we say our pleases. We ask him for the things we want or need. And when we're all done, when it's time to stop, we close in the name of the Savior and say, 'Amen.' So it's, 'In the name of Jesus Christ. Amen.' Beyond that, it's just what's in your heart. You're talking to your Father; you just say what comes."

"But I don't know about thees and thous. It's like Shakespeare, and I don't know anything about that."

"That's okay. It will come in time, but it doesn't make much difference. God will understand what you mean. So will you pray for us? I'm getting a feeling like a prayer would do us some good. Give us a Christmas prayer, my brother, to make our holiday complete."

The SAW gunner muttered in the affirmative, let go

of his rifle on the floor beside him, and brought his hands together on his chest, the fingers erect and against one another, his eyes closed.

"Dear Heavenly Father," he said and then paused briefly. "Thank you for Jesus. Thank you for giving him to us. Thank you for letting him die for us. Thank you for all the people who believe in him. Thank you for my friend who has been here helping me today. Thank you for these two brave men who died here today. Thank you for the United States of America and for the land of the free. Thank you that we could wear our country's uniform and defend our country's flag. Thank you that we could help these people be free. Thank you that I could learn more about Jesus and about you. Thank you for the prayer that was said on me today. Thank you for all my family and friends. Thank you for that sandwich the corporal made for me."

It wasn't gratuitous crying. It wasn't sobbing. It wasn't wailing. It was the tender tears of a broken and grateful heart. The tears of a peaceable follower of Christ. The tears of a man who's not behind a wall anymore.

"I ask you to take the corporal and the specialist to heaven. I ask you to take care of their families and make them not hurt too bad. I ask you that I will be able to see my mother when I die. I ask you that we won't get killed. I ask you that help will come and save us. I ask you that these people will stop being like this, that they won't be mad anymore, that they will just go about their business and let us go about our business and we can stop having a war. I ask you to keep our country safe and free. I ask you to protect all our troops, that they can do their missions and go home to their families. I ask you that I can keep loving Jesus. I ask you that I can live the way I'm supposed to live. I ask you that I can learn what I have to learn and be the man I'm supposed to be. I ask you that we can all live in peace and people can just get married and have kids and there won't be any more evil in the world. I ask you that my dad won't miss me. I ask that you will be happy with me. I ask that Jesus will always be with me. I ask that whoever's sick won't be sick anymore. I ask that everybody will have a merry Christmas. In the name of Jesus Christ. Amen."

"Amen," the grenadier whispered. That was in a ramshackle nowhere store with a kicked in door, blown-out windows, two dead GIs on the floor, a scattering of dead townies outside, a Humvee blown to smithereens, and a couple of young followers of Christ expecting to die.

"I know that these things are true," the grenadier said. "I know that God lives and loves us. I know he is really our father. I know that Jesus is the Christ. That he is our elder brother. That he died for us. And that because of him we can return and live again with our Heavenly Father. I know that the heavens have been opened, that God speaks to man, that the gospel has been restored and that everything we need to save ourselves and our families is on the earth today."

"I know that too," the SAW gunner said. "I know there's a God. I know there's a Jesus. I know he came back from the dead. I know he's going to take me to heaven. I know he brought you to me. I know he's kept us alive today. I know I want to learn more about him. I know that I feel better than I ever have in my life."

The grenadier was late for his webcam now, and back at a little apartment in Watertown his wife sat in front of the computer waiting for him to show up on her buddy list. The baby was sleeping in the crib in the footy pajamas with the proud All-American emblem of the 82nd Airborne. It was her first Christmas alone away from family, and the northern New York winter was already wetter and more miserable than the ones she had known in Cache Valley. There hadn't been enough money for her to go home to be with family for the holidays, and she probably should have just moved home to stay while he was deployed. But it was important that they have a place of their own, so in their four rooms she sat alone in a folding chair watching the buddy list with her baby asleep across the room two hours after he was supposed to log on. The tree on the corner table was white-flocked aluminum decorated with pictures from their wedding, pictures she had glued to construction paper and edged with her scrapbooking scissors. For no particular reason she began to cry.

The grenadier low-crawled over to the corporal, undid his cargo pocket, and pulled out the digital camera, which he found in working order. Then he took it over to the SAW gunner and said they had to get a picture. He bent down so his face was next to the SAW gunner's, and as he held the camera out at arm's length, they both put on big wide-grin smiles and gave the thumbs-up. Then the SAW gunner took a picture of the grenadier holding up the hand sign that the specialist had made and passed the camera over to the grenadier, who took a picture of the SAW gunner doing the same thing. The grenadier worked back to the corporal, returned the camera to its pocket, crossed the man's hands on his chest, and pulled his dog tags out of his shirt so they were visible. He did the same thing for the specialist and pulled his head back from the extreme tilt it had been in for CPR.

"I liked those guys," the SAW gunner said.

"Yeah, they seemed like pretty nice guys," the grenadier said.

He was back on his case of oil now. He rechecked the magazines he had gathered up and slung one of the extra M16s on his back as a reserve in case his jammed. He sat there with his rifle across his knees, locked and loaded, waiting.

"It ought to be about another hour," the grenadier said. "The sun will be down by then. Remember what I said about those grenades."

"I gotcha, brother," the SAW gunner said. "I frag

anybody who's not a Yankees fan."

He was in a bad way, the grenadier knew. A person can only lose so much blood, a person can only last so long without help, and a person can only endure so much. And the man with the riddled leg was on borrowed time. There was a chance, the grenadier thought, that he would be gone before the attack came. Probably passed out, maybe dead. Maybe the cold and the falling blood pressure to his brain would overcome him. Maybe this had all been delayed in order to ease him over to the other side. Maybe that's what God was thinking. Then something came to him.

"Hey," he said to the SAW gunner, "I forgot to give you your Christmas present." He unbuttoned his left cargo pocket, opposite the one that held the little New Testament, and brought out a small, dark-red book with gold lettering. He'd gotten it for four dollars at the Distribution Center across from the Humanitarian Center. "This is another witness of Jesus Christ. Read this and you'll do okay." He flung it across the room, and it landed on the floor, sliding to a stop against the SAW gunner's M16. The injured man picked it up, riffled the pages, said he'd read it, and tucked it inside his vest.

The street was dead quiet. Nothing was moving. Even the afternoon birds weren't lighting.

The grenadier pulled out the New Testament and a pen and opened the little book to the page with the flag, and writing in small letters in the white space, he wrote a letter to his infant son. "Take care of your mommy," he wrote, "she is a wonderful woman. And please know that all through your life I will be," and then he stopped. He sniffed like he had that one time before, blinked, and put the pen back on the paper and thought, *I will be. I will be. I will be.* And then he wrote, "right there beside you." He thought he'd finish it later, and he stuffed the book back in his cargo pocket and set the pen down.

Then he picked it up again and held his left palm out flat and hard and wrote something on it. Two words. Names. "Aubrey" and "Gordon." Switching the pen to his left hand he held out his right palm and wrote something on it. A reference: Helaman 5:12.

He put the pen away, regripped his rifle, and looked over at the bloodied and broken man he had met three weeks ago.

"Merry Christmas, my friend," the SAW gunner slurred.

"Merry Christmas, my friend," the grenadier answered. "Glory to God in the highest, and on Earth peace, good will toward men."

"Amen," whispered the SAW gunner.

There was silence, and the grenadier stared out the window at the buildings on the far side of the road, working his eyes methodically up and down the street. He held the M16 ready in his hands.

And then he began to sing—softly, plaintively, beautifully.

"I know that my Redeemer lives. What comfort this sweet sentence gives! He lives, he lives, who once was dead. He lives, my everliving Head. He lives to bless me with his love. He lives to plead for me above. He lives my hungry soul to feed. He lives to bless in time of need." Then he hummed a bit. "He lives to silence all my fears. He lives to wipe away my tears. He lives to calm my troubled heart. He lives all blessings to impart." More humming. And then just talking. "He lives and grants me daily breath. He lives and I shall conquer death."

To the left of the Humvee, a cat suddenly ran out of a courtyard.

The grenadier then began to sing "A Poor Wayfaring Man of Grief," but he realized that he didn't know the words, so he took up "Come, Come, Ye Saints," joining it in the middle. "Why should we mourn, or think our lot is hard? 'Tis not so; all is right. Why should we think to earn a great reward if we now shun the fight? Gird up your loins; fresh courage take. Our God will never us forsake; And soon we'll have this tale to tell—All is well! All is well!"

And they moved. All along the far side of the street. Easily a dozen of them. From every door and courtyard and alley. Men with Kalashnikovs. At a dead sprint. And he leapt up, electric, one stride and then a second and then a hurdle through where the window had been, and from where the SAW gunner lay, he glimpsed the grenadier charge forward with his finger on the trigger of the M203, and he heard the throaty boom of its explosive charge, the constant snare drum rat-a-tat-tat of the Kalashnikovs, and the repeated bursts of three from an M16. A spraying of fire one way and then another. And a wide-open lot with no cover for anyone—just a kill zone in a hurry. And the SAW gunner held the tang of his first grenade against the palm of his hand as he pulled the pin and waited.

He listened for the M16 but couldn't make it out. Then the firing stopped altogether, and he heard men running and the sound of voices. Foreign voices. He waited for the men to get closer, and he could hear them approaching the front of the store. When he thought he could almost see them, he lobbed the fragmentation grenade over the cinder block wall. When it went off a moment later, the concussion knocked the air from his lungs and made his ears ring and bleed, and the blast and the dust dominated everything.

There was quiet and moaning and at the end of the street suddenly the sound of more gunfire. Big heavy gunfire. Urgent gunfire that escalated rapidly near what sounded like the middle of the street and then petered out in small shots here and there along what must have been the street and the buildings that lined it. Running footfalls crossed the gravel lot in front of the store, approaching it, and the SAW gunner shouted out, "Who goes there?"

There was a confused scatter of gravel where the boots

instantly stopped. An eighteen-year-old with a Southern accent responded, "United States Army. Who goes there?"

"United States Army. Come on in," the SAW gunner replied.

He was putting the pin back in the second grenade when the Southern kid and his fire team came through the front door and looked down at him.

"Merry Christmas, GI Joe," the SAW gunner said.

"Merry Christmas, buddy," the Southern kid's corporal said. "This is the best day of your life. You get to go home."

"Amen," the SAW gunner whispered. "I *do* get to go home."

(circa 1984)

ABOUT THE AUTHOR

Bob Lonsberry is a radio talk show host who has also worked as a newspaper columnist and reporter. He served a mission for The Church of Jesus Christ of Latter-day Saints on and around the Indian reservations of the American Southwest.

A decorated veteran of the United States Army, he lives in Mount Morris, New York, which is the birthplace of Francis Bellamy, the author of the Pledge of Allegiance. He is married and is the father of five children.

0 26575 79711 4